CILANTRO

CILANTRO

A BOOK OF RECIPES

HELEN SUDELL

LORENZ BOOKS

This edition is published by Lorenz Books
an imprint of Anness Publishing Limited
Blaby Road, Wigston, Leicestershire LE18 4SE
info@anness.com

www.lorenzbooks.com; www.annesspublishing.com

If you like the images in this book and would like to
investigate using them for publishing, promotions
or advertising, please visit our website
www.practicalpictures.com for more information

A CIP catalogue record for this book is available from
The British Library

Publisher Joanna Lorenz
Editorial Director Helen Sudell
Designer Nigel Partridge
Illustrations Anna Koska

Recipes by: Mridula Baljekar, Ghillie Basan, Judy Bastyra,
Miguel de Castro e Silva, Matthew Drennan, Silvana
Franco, Lasley Mackley, Linda Tubby, Jenny White
Photographers Martin Brigdale, Nicki Dowey, William
Lingwood, Craig Robertson, Jon Whitaker
Jacket photography Janine Hosegood

COOK'S NOTES
• Bracketed terms are intended for American readers.
• For all recipes, quantities are given in both metric and
imperial measures and, where appropriate, in standard
cups and spoons. Follow one set of measures, but not a
mixture, because they are not interchangeable.
• Standard spoon and cup measures are level. 1 tsp = 5ml,
1 tbsp = 15ml, 1 cup = 250ml/8fl oz.
• Australian standard tablespoons are 20ml. Australian
readers should use 3 tsp in place of 1 tbsp for measuring
small quantities.
• American pints are 16fl oz/2 cups. American readers
should use 20fl oz/2.5 cups in place of 1 pint when
measuring liquids.
• Electric oven temperatures in this book are for
conventional ovens. When using a fan oven, the
temperature will probably need to be reduced by about
10–20°C/20–40°F. Since ovens vary, you should check
with your manufacturer's instruction book for guidance.
• The nutritional analysis given for each recipe is calculated
per portion (i.e. serving or item), unless otherwise stated.
If the recipe gives a range, such as Serves 4–6, then the
nutritional analysis will be for the smaller portion size,
i.e. 6 servings. The analysis does not include optional
ingredients, such as salt added to taste.
• Medium (US large) eggs are used unless
otherwise stated.

PUBLISHER'S NOTE

CONTENTS

INTRODUCTION

Coriander, or cilantro, has always been highly esteemed in the East and in Mediterranean countries, where it has been used for thousands of years. Now, thanks to the influence of Thai and Indian restaurants and the popularity of Mexican food, Westerners have taken to it with a vengeance. The smell and flavour of fresh coriander is almost indescribable – you are

Below: Fresh coriander (cilantro) is a popular garnish.

either addicted to it, or would travel miles to avoid it. Coriander can be described as pungent and exotic, almost astringent, with a touch of citrus and cumin.

In America, the fresh herb is known as cilantro (from the Spanish culantro). Confusingly, the coriander plant is also known as Chinese parsley, though it bears about as much resemblance to parsley as mint.

Coriander is a wonderfully versatile plant. The leaves, stems, roots and seeds can all be used to create slightly different flavours.

In regions as diverse as India, China, South-east Asia, Latin America, Portugal and the Middle East, fresh coriander appears in all kinds of dishes either as a flavouring or garnish. It adds wonderful vibrancy and freshness to stews, curries, salads, soups, relishes, stir-fries, bean and chilli dishes. In Mexican and Asian cooking,

Above: The seeds can be dry-fried or ground.

coriander, lime and chillies form a magical trinity which lifts even the most simple seafood and salad to the realms of gastronomic euphoria.

Fresh coriander root is one of the key ingredients in Thai food, and gives it that unmistakable characteristic flavour. The root is pounded with garlic and black pepper to make a potent marinade for meat or fish, or it may be dried and ground and used as a key ingredient in curry pastes.

Coriander seed is used in Indian and South-east Asian dishes where it adds an enticingly warm earthy flavour to curries, spice mixtures, marinades, relishes and fresh chutneys. It is also used in classic French marinated vegetable dishes.

The recipes in this book draw on exotic cuisines to enable you to experience the versatility of this plant. They begin with a mouthwatering

Below: The fresh herb is a key ingredient in spicy salsas.

selection of soups, starters and snacks, and then go on to fish and seafood dishes, with which fresh coriander is particularly delicious. The section on meat and poultry demonstrates the different flavours of the seed and the leaf. Finally, anyone left

Above: Grow herbs on a sunny windowsill for instant access.

in any doubt will be won over by the inspiring selection of assertively flavoured vegetable and side dishes plus a choice of beautifully spiced breads.

TYPES OF CORIANDER

CORIANDER (CILANTRO) PLANT

The upper leaves of the plant are delicate and feathery; the lower leaves are broader and finely scalloped, similar in appearance to flat leaf parsley. Use the lower leaves whole as a garnish, or add to dishes towards the end of cooking time for a wonderfully exotic flavour. Chopped leaves can also be used in salads, soups, curries, sauces and dips. Fresh coriander is also delicious in chutneys to accompany spicy dishes, and is a popular ingredient for salsas.

FRESH CORIANDER ROOT

When you buy a bunch of fresh coriander leaves, check that the roots are still attached. They not only help keep the leaves fresher but are also a useful ingredient themselves. The roots should be washed and sliced, then choppped or pounded, and added to Thai-style meat or poultry curries, stir-fries and marinades, or add to other root vegetables in stews and casseroles.

CORIANDER SEED

Life the leaf, coriander seed has a distinctive, pungent, spicy, flavour. The colours of the seeds range from green to cream and brown. Use them whole, or crush as required. To bring out the warm, earthy flavour, dry-fry in a heavy-based pan for a few minutes before crushing. Commercially ground coriander seed has a fragrant aroma and a pleasant taste, mild and sweet yet slightly pungent.

CORIANDER PASTE

Made from fresh coriander (cilantro) pounded with oil, salt and acetic acid, commercially produced coriander paste is a convenient substitute, but it lacks the flavour of the fresh leaf. It can be stored in the refrigerator for at least 12 months after opening .

MEDICINAL USES OF CORIANDER

The leaves and seeds have digestive properties and stimulate appetite. The essential oil has fungicidal and antibacterial properties. In traditional Indian medicine decoctions of the seeds were taken as a small-pox preventive. They are still considered helpful in lowering blood cholesterol levels.

Coriander plant

Ground coriander

Coriander seed

Coriander paste

Coriander (cilantro) leaves

Fresh coriander root

COOKING WITH CORIANDER

Fresh coriander (cilantro) leaves have a stronger, spicier taste than the seeds, which are milder and sweeter.

PREPARING FRESH CORIANDER (CILANTRO)

It is important to use leaves that are as fresh as possible. Discard any wilted leaves.

Removing stalks: Pinch off the upper leaves from the stalks so that a minimum amount of stalk is still attached. Then pinch off the pair of leaves which grow further down the stalk. Discard any tough stalks. Wash the leaves and dry in a salad spinner or on paper towels.

Chopping: Fresh herbs can be chopped coarsely or finely depending on personal preference, and according to the dish they are to be used in. Gather the herbs into a tight clump with one hand while you chop with the other. Then chop with both hands on the knife until they are sufficiently fine.

Puréeing: Remove and discard any tough stalks from 75g/3oz

fresh coriander, and roughly chop the leaves by hand. Put the chopped leaves in a blender with 30ml/1 tbsp each of lime juice and olive oil. Season to taste. Purée for 3 minutes, scraping the sides of the bowl frequently to ensure an even mix.

Freezing: A useful way to capture the flavours of summer through the winter months is to freeze herbs. Finely chop a generous amount of fresh coriander and freeze in ice cube trays. The frozen cubes can be added directly to dishes. Don't use frozen coriander as a garnish as the texture deteriorates when defrosted.

PREPARING CORIANDER SEEDS

Coriander seeds are the principal flavouring agent in many curries. For maximum flavour, use freshly toasted and ground seeds. Frying the ground seeds in oil before adding other ingredients releases even more flavour and gives the finished dish a distinctive 'curry' taste.

Dry-frying seeds: To bring out the aroma dry-fry the seeds without any oil in a heavy-based pan. Stir frequently and be careful not to let them burn.

Grinding toasted seeds: Crush coriander seeds in a mortar with a pestle, or grind them to a powder using a coffee grinder kept just for this purpose.

Above: Chop fresh leaves as and when you need them.

BUYING FRESH CORIANDER

Choose robust, green, fresh-looking leaves. Avoid any that look limp, yellow or bruised as they will quickly start to rot. Avoid bunches that have a large proportion of feathery upper leaves – they have probably bolted and the flavour will be affected. Coriander will last longer if you buy it with the roots still attached. Chinese or Thai stores are a good source.

Above: A sunny windowsill is an ideal spot to grow the herb.

GROWING CORIANDER

Coriander is a hardy annual that is easy to grow either in well prepared ground or in a pot on the kitchen windowsill. As it doesn't like being moved once planted it is better to sow the seeds in situ in late spring once the ground has warmed up. It will grow best in well-drained, fertile soil with ample water in the early stages, followed by warmth and sunshine. Keep well watered during dry spells.

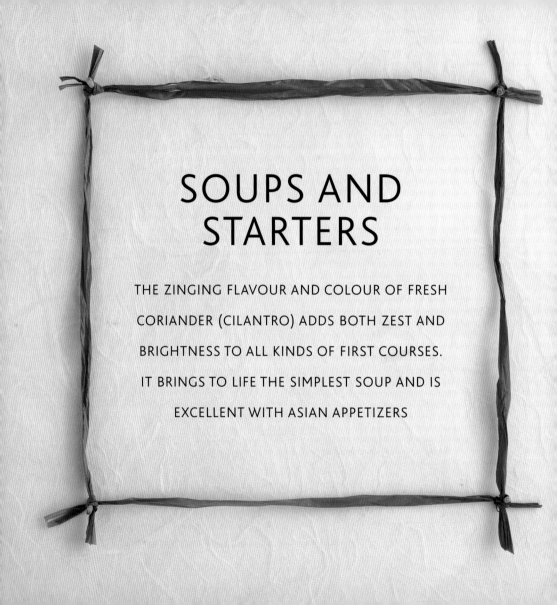

SOUPS AND STARTERS

THE ZINGING FLAVOUR AND COLOUR OF FRESH

CORIANDER (CILANTRO) ADDS BOTH ZEST AND

BRIGHTNESS TO ALL KINDS OF FIRST COURSES.

IT BRINGS TO LIFE THE SIMPLEST SOUP AND IS

EXCELLENT WITH ASIAN APPETIZERS

CARROT AND CORIANDER SOUP

Root vegetables, such as carrots, are great for soups. Their earthy flavour becomes rich and sweet when cooked slowly over a gentle heat and goes perfectly with robust herbs and spices.

Serves 4

15ml/1 tbsp sunflower oil
40g/1½oz/3 tbsp butter
1 onion, chopped
1 stick celery, thinly sliced, plus 2–3 pale leafy tops
2 small potatoes, peeled and chopped
450g/1lb carrots, cut into chunks
900ml/1½ pints/3¾ cups boiling vegetable stock
10ml/2 tsp ground coriander
15ml/1 tbsp chopped fresh coriander (cilantro)
150ml/¼ pint/⅔ cup milk
salt and ground black pepper

Energy 168Kcal/697kJ; Protein 3g;
Carbohydrate 11.9g, of which sugars 9.2g;
Fat 12.4g, of which saturates 6g;
Cholesterol 24mg; Calcium 94mg; Fibre
3.1g; Sodium 758mg.

Heat the oil and 25g/1oz/2 tbsp of the butter in a pan and gently fry the onion for 3–4 minutes. Add the celery and potatoes to the pan. Cook for 2 minutes, add the carrots and cook for a further 1 minute.

Pour the boiling vegetable stock over the vegetables, then season. Cover and simmer on low for 40 minutes until the vegetables are tender.

Melt the remaining butter in a large pan and add the ground coriander. Fry for about 1 minute, stirring constantly, until the aromas are released. Reduce the heat and add the fresh coriander. Fry for about 30 seconds, then remove the pan from the heat.

Process the soup in a food processor or blender until smooth, then pour into the pan with the coriander. Stir in the milk and heat gently until piping hot. Check the seasoning, then serve garnished with the reserved celery leaves.

CORIANDER CREAM WITH CHEESE AND TOMATO CONFIT

This creamy soup is usually served warm, but it is just as delicious cold. It is the perfect choice as a chilled appetizer for an al fresco meal.

Serves 4

90ml/6 tbsp olive oil
3 onions, halved and sliced
1 garlic clove, chopped
2 bunches of fresh coriander
    (cilantro), about 300g/11oz,
    chopped
300g/11oz potatoes, diced
8 cherry tomatoes, peeled
150g/5oz feta cheese, cut into
    cubes
salt and ground black pepper

Heat half the oil in a large pan. Add the onion, garlic and coriander and cook over a low heat, stirring occasionally, for 5 minutes, until softened.

Add the potatoes and 1 litre/1¾ pints/4 cups water. Bring to the boil, then lower the heat and cook for 20–30 minutes, until the potatoes are tender. Meanwhile, preheat the oven to 160°C/325°F/Gas 3.

Transfer the soup to a food processor or blender and process to a purée. Season to taste with salt. If you are serving the soup hot, reheat gently. Otherwise, leave to cool, then chill in the refrigerator.

Place the tomatoes in a small casserole, drizzle them with the remaining olive oil and season with salt and pepper. Bake the tomatoes in the oven for 10 minutes.

Serve the soup hot or cold in bowls with two tomatoes each, the cubed cheese and sprinkled with some of the olive oil used to cook the tomatoes.

VARIATION

If you choose to serve this soup hot, try replacing the feta cheese with cubes of cured goat's cheese, warmed in the oven and sprinkled over at the last minute, as a delicious alternative.

Energy 353kcal/1467kJ; Protein 11.6g; Carbohydrate 23.6g, of which sugars 9.5g; Fat 24.3g, of which saturates 8.8g; Cholesterol 35mg; Calcium 137mg; Fibre 4g; Sodium 247mg.

CRAB AND CHILLI SOUP WITH FRESH CORIANDER RELISH

Prepared fresh crab is readily available, high quality and convenient – perfect for creating an exotic soup in minutes. Here it is accompanied by a hot coriander (cilantro) and chilli relish.

Serves 4

45ml/3 tbsp olive oil
1 red onion, finely chopped
2 red chillies, seeded and finely chopped
1 garlic clove, finely chopped
450g/1lb fresh white crab meat
30ml/2 tbsp chopped fresh parsley
30ml/2 tbsp chopped fresh coriander (cilantro)
juice of 2 lemons
1 lemon grass stalk
1 litre/1¾ pints/4 cups fish stock
15ml/1 tbsp Thai fish sauce (nam pla)
150g/5oz vermicelli
salt and ground black pepper

For the coriander relish

1 green chilli
50g/2oz/1 cup fresh coriander (cilantro) leaves
15ml/1 tbsp sunflower oil
25ml/1½ tbsp lemon juice
2.5ml/½ tsp ground roasted cumin seeds

Heat the oil in a saucepan and add the onion, chillies and garlic. Cook over a gentle heat for 10 minutes until the onion is very soft. Transfer this mixture to a bowl and stir in the crab meat, parsley, coriander and lemon juice, then set aside.

Lay the lemon grass on a chopping board and bruise it with a rolling pin or pestle. Pour the stock and fish sauce into a saucepan. Add the lemon grass and bring to the boil. Break the pasta into 7.5cm/3in lengths and add to the boiling water. Simmer, uncovered, for 3–4 minutes or according to the packet instructions, until the pasta is just tender.

Meanwhile, make the coriander relish. Deseed and finely chop the green chilli. Place the fresh coriander, chilli, oil, lemon juice and cumin in a food processor or blender and process to form a coarse paste (or use a mortar and pestle). Add seasoning to taste.

Remove and discard the lemon grass from the soup. Stir the chilli and crab mixture into the soup and season it well. Bring to the boil, then reduce the heat and simmer for 2 minutes.

Ladle the soup into four deep, warmed bowls and put a spoonful of the relish in the centre of each. Serve at once.

Energy 228kcal/951kj; Protein 23.6g; Carbohydrate 5.4g; of which sugars 5g; Fat 12.6g; of which saturates 6g; Cholesterol 90mg; Calcium 199mg; Fibre 1.1g; Sodium 767mg.

LEBANESE CHICKPEA DIP

This classic dip can, of course, be bought ready-made, but made at home it can be varied widely to taste – some enjoy it spiked with cumin, garlic or chilli; others prefer it light and lemony.

Serves 4–6

225g/8oz dried chickpeas, soaked in water for at least 6 hours, or overnight
45–60ml/3–4 tbsp olive oil
1–2 cloves garlic, crushed
juice of 1 lemon
juice of 1 Seville orange, or ½ large orange
45–60ml/3–4 tbsp tahini
sea salt and freshly ground black pepper
pitta bread or crudités, to serve

To garnish
15ml/1 tbsp olive oil
small bunch of fresh coriander (cilantro), finely chopped

Energy 265kcal/1101kJ; Protein 10g; Carbohydrate 12.6g, of which sugars 0.8g; Fat 19.7g, of which saturates 2.8g; Cholesterol 0mg; Calcium 210mg; Fibre 4.7g; Sodium 15mg

Drain the chickpeas and place them in a pan with plenty of water. Bring to the boil, reduce the heat and simmer, covered, for about 1½ hours, until the chickpeas are very soft. Drain, reserving a few spoonfuls of the cooking liquid, and remove any loose skins. Put the chickpeas and liquid into a blender or food processor.

Whizz the chickpeas to a thick purée. Add the olive oil, garlic, lemon and orange juices and tahini and blend thoroughly. Season with salt and pepper to taste.

Turn the hummus into a serving bowl and drizzle a little oil over the surface to keep it moist. Sprinkle with a little coriander and serve with strips of warm pitta bread or crudités such as carrot, celery and (bell) pepper sticks.

GUACAMOLE

This dish has almost become a cliché of Tex-Mex cooking, usually served as a first course with bread or corn chips for dipping. It is a great accompaniment for simple grilled fish, poultry or meat.

Serves 4

2 large ripe avocados
1 small red onion, very finely
    chopped
1 red or green chilli, seeded and
    very finely chopped
½–1 garlic clove, crushed with a
    little salt (optional)
finely shredded rind (zest) of ½
    lime and juice of 1–1½ limes
pinch of caster (superfine) sugar
225g/8oz tomatoes, seeded
    and chopped
30ml/2 tbsp roughly chopped
    fresh coriander (cilantro)
2.5–5ml/½–1 tsp ground
    toasted cumin seeds
15ml/1 tbsp olive oil
15–30ml/1–2 tbsp soured
    cream (optional)
salt and ground black pepper
lime wedges, dipped in sea salt,
    and fresh coriander (cilantro)
    sprigs, to garnish

Halve, stone and peel the avocados. Set one half aside and roughly mash the remainder in a bowl using a fork.

Add the onion, chilli, garlic (if using), lime rind, juice of 1 lime, sugar, tomatoes and coriander. Add the ground cumin seeds, seasoning and more lime juice to taste. Stir in the olive oil.

Dice the remaining avocado and stir into the guacamole, then cover and leave to stand for 15 minutes so that the flavour develops. Stir in the soured cream, if using. Serve immediately with lime wedges, dipped in sea salt, and coriander sprigs.

Energy 244kcal/1010kJ; Protein 8.8g; Carbohydrate 4.4g, of which sugars 4.3g; Fat 21.4g, of which saturates 8.5g; Cholesterol 35mg; Calcium 205mg; Fibre 0.7g; Sodium 731mg

CARROT AND CORIANDER SOUFFLÉS

Depending on how it is used, coriander (cilantro) can give a robust or a delicate flavour. Here, it perfectly complements carrot in this light-as-air dish.

Serves 4

450 g/1 lb carrots
30 ml/2 tbsp fresh chopped coriander (cilantro)
4 eggs, separated
salt and freshly ground black pepper

COOK'S TIP
For the best results use tender young carrots in this simple dish.

Energy 132cal/547KJ; Protein 8.4g;
Carbohydrate 9.0gm, of which sugars
8.5g; Fats 7.1gm, of which saturates 2g;
Cholesterol 231.0mg; Calcium 69.8mg;
Fibre 2.7g; Sodium 114mg.

Peel the carrots and thinly slice.

Cook in boiling salted water for 20 minutes or until the carrots are tender. Drain, and process until smooth in a food processor.

Preheat the oven to 200°C / 400°F /Gas Mark 6. Season the puréed carrots well, and stir in the chopped coriander. Fold the egg yolks into the carrot mixture.

In a separate bowl, whisk the egg whites until stiff. Fold the egg whites into the carrot mixture and pour into four greased ramekins. Bake for about 20 minutes or until risen and golden. Serve immediately.

EGGS ON SPICED POTATOES

The inspiration for this recipe comes from ancient Persia. This is a healthier version of the original recipe as the potatoes are shallow-fried rather than deep-fried.

Serves 4

700g/1½lb potatoes, peeled and thinly sliced
4 tbsp sunflower oil or olive oil
1 medium onion, finely chopped
1–2 green chillies, finely chopped (seeded if you like)
5ml/1 tsp salt or to taste
15g/½oz coriander (cilantro) leaves and stalks, finely chopped
4 large eggs
2.5ml/½ tsp chilli powder or paprika
2.5ml/½ tsp ground cumin

Energy 303kcal/1270kJ; Protein 9.6g; Carbohydrate 29.7g, of which sugars 3.2g; Fat 17.2g, of which saturates 3.1g; Cholesterol 190mg; Calcium 52mg; Fibre 2.2g; Sodium 91mg.

Cut the potato slices into strips about the size of thin French fries. Wash the potatoes and dry thoroughly with a clean cloth.

In a non-stick sauté pan, heat the oil over a medium heat and fry the onion and chillies for 5–6 minutes, until the onions begin to brown.

Add the potatoes and salt. Stir and mix well, then cover the pan and cook for 10–12 minutes. Stir occasionally and reduce the heat for the last 2–3 minutes. The potatoes should brown slightly.

Stir in the coriander leaves and smooth the surface by gently pressing down the potatoes.

Break the eggs on top of the potatoes, spacing them out evenly. Reduce the heat to low, cover the pan and cook for 6–7 minutes or until the eggs are set. Remove the pan from the heat and sprinkle the chilli powder or paprika and cumin over the surface. Serve immediately.

FISH AND SEAFOOD

WITH ITS DISTINCTIVE AROMA, CORIANDER

(CILANTRO) IS DELICIOUS WITH FISH AND

SEAFOOD, PARTICULARLY WHEN COMBINED WITH

THE CLEAN, ASTRINGENT FLAVOURS OF OTHER

AROMATICS SUCH AS LIMES, CHILLIES, GINGER,

AND LEMON GRASS

CLAMS WITH FRESH CORIANDER

This method of cooking is one of the most effective ways to enjoy the flavour of clams. For a more substantial main dish, add butter beans and mashed tomato and serve with crusty bread.

Serves 4

600g/1lb 6oz live clams
100ml/3½fl oz/scant ½ cup olive oil
2 garlic cloves, very finely chopped
1 lemon
1 bunch of fresh coriander (cilantro), chopped

COOK'S TIP
All shellfish deteriorates very rapidly once out of the sea. Buy clams from a reputable supplier and cook them on the day of purchase. It is unwise to collect clams from the beach because of the risk of pollution.

Scrub the clams under cold running water. Discard any with broken shells or that do not shut immediately when sharply tapped.

Heat the olive oil in a large, heavy pan. Add the clams and garlic, cover with a tight-fitting lid and cook, shaking the pan frequently, for 3–5 minutes, until the shells open. Discard any that remain closed.

Halve the lemon and then squeeze the juice from one half into a bowl. Cut the other lemon half into wedges. Add the coriander and lemon juice to the clams and serve immediately with the lemon wedges.

Energy 197kcal/816kJ; Protein 8.9g; Carbohydrate 2.3g, of which sugars 0.4g; Fat 17g, of which saturates 2.5g; Cholesterol 34mg; Calcium 63mg; Fibre 0.9g; Sodium 605mg.

PATRA NI MACCHI

This Indian recipe translates as fish in a leaf parcel. The gutsy flavour of salmon is coated in a richly spiced coconut and coriander (cilantro) paste and then steamed over a barbecue.

Serves 6

50g/2oz fresh coconut, skinned and finely grated, or 65g/2½oz/scant 1 cup desiccated (dry unsweetened shredded) coconut, soaked in 30ml/2 tbsp water

1 large lemon, skin, pith and seeds removed, roughly chopped

4 large garlic cloves, crushed

3 large fresh mild green chillies, seeded and chopped

50g/2oz fresh coriander (cilantro), roughly chopped

25g/1oz fresh mint leaves, roughly chopped

5ml/1 tsp ground cumin

5ml/1 tsp sugar

2.5ml/½ tsp fenugreek seeds, finely ground

5ml/1 tsp salt

2 large, whole banana leaves

6 salmon fillets, total weight about 1.2kg/2½lb, skinned

Place all the ingredients except the banana leaves and salmon in a food processor. Pulse to a fine paste. Scrape the mixture into a bowl, cover and chill for 30 minutes.

Prepare the barbecue. While it is heating, make the parcels. Cut each banana leaf widthways into three and cut off the hard outside edge from each piece. Put the pieces of leaf and the edge strips in a bowl of hot water. Leave to soak for about 10 minutes. Drain, gently wipe off any white residue, rinse the leaves and strips, and pour over boiling water to soften. Drain, then place the leaves, smooth-side up, on a clean board.

Smear the top and bottom of each salmon fillet with the coconut paste. Place one fillet on each banana leaf. Bring the trimmed edge of the leaf over the salmon, then fold in the sides. Finally, bring up the remaining edge to cover the salmon and make a neat parcel. Tie each parcel securely with a leaf strip.

Lay each parcel on a sheet of heavy-duty foil, bring up the edges and scrunch the tops together to seal. Once the flames have died down, position a lightly oiled grill rack over the coals to heat. When the coals are medium-hot, or with a moderate coating of ash, place the salmon parcels on the grill rack and cook for about 8-12 minutes, turning over once.

Place on individual plates and leave to stand for 2–3 minutes – the salmon will continue to cook in the residual heat of the parcel. Remove the foil, then unwrap and eat the fish straight out of the leaf parcel.

Energy 567kcal/2349kJ; Protein 34.9g; Carbohydrate 1g, of which sugars 0.8g; Fat 47.1g, of which saturates 7.5g; Cholesterol 113mg; Calcium 64mg; Fibre 0.6g; Sodium 1723mg.

SCALLOPS WITH GARLIC AND CORIANDER

Shellfish is best cooked very simply. In this light and fragrant dish, hot chilli sauce and lime add piquancy and vibrancy which perfectly complement the rich scallops.

Serves 4

20 scallops
2 courgettes (zucchini)
75g/3oz/6 tbsp butter
15ml/1 tbsp vegetable oil
4 garlic cloves, chopped
30ml/2 tbsp hot chilli sauce
juice of 1 lime
small bunch of fresh coriander,
  (cilantro) finely chopped

COOK'S TIP

Most scallops are sold pre-shucked. However if buying fresh scallops only purchase ones that have tightly closed shells or that close their shell when you tap them. Discard any that do not do this.

If you have bought scallops in their shells, open them. Hold a scallop shell in the palm of your hand, with the flat side uppermost. Insert the blade of a knife close to the hinge that joins the shells and prise them apart. Run the blade of the knife across the inside of the flat shell to cut away the scallop. Only the white adductor muscle and the orange coral are eaten, so pull away and discard all other parts. Rinse the scallops under cold running water.

Cut the courgettes in half, then into four pieces lengthways. Melt the butter in the oil in a large frying pan. Add the courgettes and fry until soft. Remove from the pan and keep warm. Add the garlic and fry until golden. Stir in the hot chilli sauce.

Add the scallops to the sauce. Cook, stirring constantly, for 1–2 minutes only. Stir in the lime juice, chopped coriander and the courgette pieces. Serve immediately on warmed plates.

Energy 291kcal/1213kJ; Protein 24.2g; Carbohydrate 4.4g, of which sugars 1g; Fat 19.8g, of which saturates 10.5g; Cholesterol 87mg; Calcium 45mg; Fibre 0.5g; Sodium 294mg..

HAKE WITH CORIANDER PESTO SALSA

This aromatic salsa tastes wonderful drizzled over fish and chicken, tossed with pasta ribbons or used to dress a fresh avocado and tomato salad. To serve as a dip, mix it with a little mayonnaise.

Serves 4

50 g/2 oz fresh coriander
   (cilantro) leaves
15 g/½ oz fresh parsley
2 red chillies
1 garlic clove
50 g/2 oz/⅓ cup shelled
   pistachio nuts
25 g/1 oz Parmesan cheese,
   finely grated
90 ml/6 tbsp olive oil
juice of 2 limes
salt and ground black pepper
30 ml/2 tbsp olive oil
4 fillets of hake or other white
   fish such as whiting or
   haddock
2 limes, quartered, to serve

VARIATION

Any number of different herbs may be used to make a similar salsa to this one – try a mixture of rosemary and parsley.

Process the fresh coriander and parsley in a blender or food processor until finely chopped.

Halve the chillies lengthways and remove their seeds. Add to the herbs together with the garlic and process until finely chopped.

Add the pistachio nuts to the herb mixture and pulse the power until they are roughly chopped. Stir in the Parmesan cheese, olive oil and lime juice and season to taste.

Spoon the mixture into a serving bowl and cover and chill until ready to serve.

Heat the olive oil in a large frying pan and add the hake fillets. Cook for 10 minutes, turning once until crisp on the outside but with tender flesh. Serve immediately with the salsa and lime quarters.

Energy 443cal/1836KJ; Protein 28.8g; Carbohydrate 4.4gm, of which sugars 4.0g; Fats 34.5gm, of which saturates 6g; Cholesterol 34.6mg; Calcium 127.8mg; Fibre 1.0g; Sodium 257mg.

POULTRY
AND MEAT

CORIANDER (CILANTRO) LEAF AND SEED

HEIGHTEN THE FLAVOUR OF ALL TYPES OF MEAT

AND POULTRY DISHES. THE FRAGRANT SPICINESS

HELPS TO TEMPER ANY RICHNESS AND IS

ESPECIALLY GOOD WITH LAMB AND CHICKEN.

CHICKEN & CORIANDER PIZZA

The addition of shiitake mushrooms adds an earthy flavour to this colourful pizza, while fresh red chilli and coriander (cilantro) adds a hint of spiciness.

Serves 3–4

60ml/4 tbsp olive oil
350g/12oz chicken breast fillets, skinned and cut into thin strips
1 bunch spring onions (scallions), sliced
1 fresh red chilli, seeded and chopped
1 red (bell) pepper, seeded and cut into thin strips
75g/3oz fresh shiitake mushrooms, wiped and sliced
salt and freshly ground black pepper
45–60ml/3–4 tbsp chopped fresh coriander (cilantro)
1 ready-made 25–30cm/ 10–12in pizza base
150g/5oz mozzarella cheese

Preheat the oven to 220°C/425°F/Gas 7. Heat 30ml/2 tbsp of the olive oil in a wok or large frying pan. Add the chicken, spring onions, chilli, red pepper and mushrooms, and stir-fry over a high heat for 2–3 minutes until the chicken is firm but still slightly pink inside. Season to taste.

Pour off any excess oil, then set aside the chicken mixture to cool. Stir the fresh coriander into the cooled chicken mixture.

Brush the pizza base with 15ml/1 tbsp of the oil. Spoon over the chicken mixture and drizzle over the remaining olive oil.

Grate the mozzarella cheese and sprinkle it evenly over the pizza. Bake on an oiled baking sheet for 15–20 minutes until crisp and golden. Serve immediately.

Energy 562cal/2359KJ; Protein 36.0g; Carbohydrate 53.8gm, of which sugars 4.0g; Fats 24.0gm, of which Sat Fat 7g; Cholesterol 83.0mg; Calcium 237.8mg; Fibre 2.2g Sodium 445mg.

LEBANESE COUSCOUS

Although couscous is most closely associated with the culinary cultures of North Africa, it is also enjoyed in Lebanon, Syria and Jordan, where it is called mograbiyeh, meaning 'from the Maghreb'.

Serves 6

450g/1lb/2½ cups couscous, rinsed and drained
30ml/2 tbsp ghee, or 30ml/ 2 tbsp olive oil with a knob of butter
1 onion, finely chopped
2–3 cloves garlic, finely chopped
1 red or green chilli, seeded and very finely chopped
1 medium carrot, finely diced
5–10ml/1–2 tsp ground cinnamon
small bunch of fresh coriander (cilantro), finely chopped
sea salt and ground black pepper

For the stock

1 small organic chicken
2 onions, quartered
2 cinnamon sticks
4 cardamom pods
4 cloves
2 bay leaves

Place the chicken in a deep pan with the other stock ingredients and cover with water. Bring the water to the boil, reduce the heat and simmer for 1 hour, or until the chicken is tender. Transfer the chicken to a plate. Strain the stock, return it to the pan and boil it over a high heat for about 30 minutes, to reduce.

Remove and discard the skin from the chicken and tear the flesh into thin strips, or cut it into bitesize chunks. Cover the chicken and keep warm.

Tip the couscous into a bowl and pour in about 500ml/17fl oz/ 2 cups warm water. Add 5ml/1 tsp salt, stir the couscous once, then place a clean dish towel over the bowl and leave for 10 minutes for the couscous to swell.

Meanwhile, heat the ghee or olive oil and butter in a heavy, shallow pan and stir in the onions and garlic. Cook for a minute to soften, then add the chilli and carrot and sauté for 2–3 minutes, until they begin to colour.

Stir the cinnamon and half the coriander into the onion mixture, then add the couscous, forking through it constantly to mix well and make sure the grains don't clump together, until it is heated through.

Turn the couscous into a warmed serving dish and arrange the shredded chicken on top. Season the reduced stock with salt and pepper and spoon some of it over the chicken to moisten. Garnish with the remaining coriander and pour the rest of the stock into a bowl for spooning over individual portions.

Energy 376kcal/1574kJ; Protein 31.9g; Carbohydrate 44.6g, of which sugars 4g; Fat 8.8g, of which saturates 3.5g; Cholesterol 70mg; Calcium 49mg; Fibre 1.1g; Sodium 128mg

CRÈME FRAÎCHE AND CORIANDER CHICKEN

Boneless chicken thighs are used for this recipe but you can substitute breast portions if you like. Be generous with the coriander (cilantro) leaves, as they have a wonderful fragrant flavour.

Serves 4

6 skinless chicken thigh fillets
15ml/1 tbsp sunflower oil
60ml/4 tbsp crème fraîche
1 small bunch of fresh coriander
*   (cilantro), roughly chopped*
salt and ground black pepper
green salad, to serve

Cut each chicken thigh into three or four pieces. Heat the oil in a large frying pan, add the chicken and cook for about 6 minutes, turning occasionally, until cooked through.

Add the crème fraîche to the pan and stir until melted, then allow to bubble for 1–2 minutes.

Add the chopped coriander to the chicken and stir to combine. Season with salt and ground black pepper to taste, and serve immediately with a green salad.

Energy 249kcal/1041kJ; Protein 32.1g; Carbohydrate 0.7g, of which sugars 0.6g; Fat 13.1g, of which saturates 5.6g; Cholesterol 174mg; Calcium 44mg; Fibre 0.6g; Sodium 143mg.

COOK'S TIP

To make a lower fat version of this dish use chicken breast portions and low-fat crème fraîche.

CHIANG MAI NOODLES

An interesting chicken dish that combines noodles with sweet, hot and sour Thai flavours. Magic paste is made from coriander, white pepper and garlic, and can be bought in Thai stores.

Serves 4

250ml/8fl oz/1 cup coconut cream
15ml/1 tbsp magic paste
5ml/1 tsp Thai red curry paste
450g/1lb chicken thigh meat, chopped into small pieces
30ml/2 tbsp dark soy sauce
2 red (bell) peppers, seeded and finely diced
600ml/1 pint/2½ cups chicken or vegetable stock
90g/3½oz fresh or dried rice noodles

For the garnishes

vegetable oil, for deep-frying
90g/3½oz fine dried rice noodles
2 pickled garlic cloves, chopped
small bunch fresh coriander (cilantro), chopped
2 limes, cut into wedges

Pour the coconut cream into a large wok or frying pan and bring to the boil over a medium heat. Continue to boil, stirring frequently, for 8–10 minutes, until the milk separates and an oily sheen appears on the surface.

Add the magic paste and red curry paste and cook, stirring constantly, for 3–5 seconds, until fragrant.

Add the chicken and toss over the heat until sealed on all sides. Stir in the soy sauce and the diced peppers and stir-fry for 3–4 minutes. Pour in the stock. Bring to the boil, then lower the heat and simmer for 10–15 minutes, until the chicken is fully cooked.

Meanwhile, make the noodle garnish. Heat the oil in a pan or deep-fryer to 190°C/375°F or until a cube of bread browns in 45 seconds. Break the fine dried noodles in half, then divide them into four portions. Add one portion at a time to the hot oil. They will puff up on contact. As soon as they are crisp, lift the noodles out with a slotted spoon and drain on kitchen paper.

Bring a large pan of water to the boil and cook the fresh or dried noodles until tender, following the instructions on the packet. Drain well, divide among four warmed individual dishes, then spoon the curry sauce over them. Top each portion with a cluster of fried noodles. Sprinkle the chopped pickled garlic and coriander over the top and serve immediately, offering lime wedges for squeezing.

Energy 245kcal/1034kJ; Protein 29.4g; Carbohydrate 27.6g, of which sugars 9g; Fat 1.8g, of which saturates 0.6g; Cholesterol 79mg; Calcium 35mg; Fibre 1.4g; Sodium 677mg.

CORIANDER BRAISED DUCK

This glorious dish requires long cooking. A pressure cooker is useful for this, but if you use one you should cook the dish without using pressure for the last half hour to concentrate the spicy juices.

Serves 6–8

1 prepared duck (about
   1.5kg/3½lb), trimmed of
   excess fat
45ml/3 tbsp vegetable oil
45g/3 tbsp minced (ground)
   onions
30g/2 tbsp garlic purée
30g/2 tbsp ground coriander
5ml/1 tsp black pepper
30ml/2 tbsp dark soy sauce
20cm/8in sugar cane, cut into 6
   pieces or 30ml/2 tbsp sugar
60ml/4 tbsp finely chopped
   fresh coriander (cilantro)
2 cinnamon sticks, 10cm/4in
   long
6 cloves
1.5 litres/2½ pints/6 cups water
8 spring onions (scallions), thinly
   sliced lengthways,
   to garnish

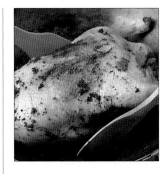 

Wash the duck and and dry it well. Heat the oil in a deep wok or pan and add the onions, garlic purée and coriander. Fry gently for 5 minutes.

Put the duck into the pan and fry for about 10 minutes, turning several times, to brown the skin all over.

Stir in all the other ingredients, cover the pan and cook over a very low heat for about 2 hours, until the duck is tender. Alternatively, transfer the duck and other ingredients to a pressure cooker and cook under high pressure for 30 minutes, then de-pressurize and braise for a further 30 minutes.

Remove the duck from the pan and keep it warm. Raise the heat and bring the sauce to a furious boil to reduce it to a syrupy consistency.

Cut the duck into large serving pieces, removing any large bones. Arrange on a serving dish and pour the sauce over it. Serve immediately with plain rice and top with sliced spring onions.

Energy 510Kcal/2120kJ; Protein 17.8g; Carbohydrate 26.9g, of which sugars 26.8g; Fat 47.5g, of which saturates 10.5g; Cholesterol 87mg; Calcium 35mg; Fibre 0.1g; Sodium 380mg.

CUMIN- AND CORIANDER-RUBBED LAMB

Rubs are quick and easy to prepare and can transform everyday cuts of meat such as chops into exciting and more unusual meals. Serve with a chunky tomato salad.

Serves 4
30ml/2 tbsp ground cumin
30ml/2 tbsp ground coriander
30ml/2 tbsp olive oil
salt and ground black pepper
8 lamb chops

Mix together the cumin, coriander and oil, and season with salt and pepper. Rub the mixture all over the lamb chops, then cover and chill for 1 hour.

Prepare a barbecue. Once the flames have died down, position a lightly oiled grill rack over the coals to heat. When the coals are medium-hot, and with a moderate coating of ash, add the chops. Cook the chops for 5 minutes on each side, until lightly charred but still pink in the centre.

Energy 494kcal/2059kJ; Protein 55.6g; Carbohydrate 0g, of which sugars 0g; Fat 30.1g, of which saturates 12.6g; Cholesterol 220mg; Calcium 18mg; Fibre 0g; Sodium 150mg.

VARIATION
To make ginger- and garlic-rubbed pork, use pork chops instead of lamb chops and substitute the cumin and coriander with ground ginger and garlic granules. Increase the cooking time to 7–8 minutes each side.

GRILLED PORK MEATBALLS

A speciality of central Vietnam, these meatballs, nem nuong, are best threaded on to skewers and grilled on a barbecue, but they can also be cooked under a grill.

Serves 4

10ml/2 tsp sesame oil
4 shallots, finely chopped
2 garlic cloves, finely chopped
450g/1lb/2 cups minced
  (ground) pork
30ml/2 tbsp nuoc mam
10ml/2 tsp five-spice powder
10ml/2 tsp sugar
salt and ground black pepper
115g/4oz/2 cups breadcrumbs
  or 30ml/2 tbsp potato starch
1 bunch of fresh coriander
  (cilantro), stalks removed

COOK'S TIP
These meatballs are usually served with noodles and a dipping sauce. You can serve them with the sauce of your choice, although in Vietnam a peanut dipping sauce is traditional.

To make the meatballs, heat the oil in a wok or small pan, and stir in the shallots and garlic. When they begin to brown, remove from the heat and leave to cool. Put the minced pork into a bowl, tip in the stir-fried shallots and garlic, and add the nuoc mam, five-spice powder and sugar. Season with a little salt and plenty of pepper. Using your hand, knead the mixture until well combined. Cover the bowl and chill in the refrigerator for 2–3 hours.

Soak eight wooden skewers in water for 30 minutes. Meanwhile, knead the mixture again, then add the breadcrumbs or potato starch, binding together well. Divide the mixture into 20 pieces and roll into balls. Thread the balls onto the skewers. Cook either over the barbecue or under the grill (broiler), turning the skewers from time to time.

Arrange the meatballs on a serving dish with coriander leaves to wrap around them, or chop the coriander and use as a garnish. Serve the meatballs hot with a peanut dipping sauce or sauce of your choice.

Energy 291Kcal/1216kJ; Protein 28g; Carbohydrate 15g, of which sugars 8g; Fat 14g, of which saturates 3g; Cholesterol 71mg; Calcium 69mg; Fibre 1.3g; Sodium 0.7g

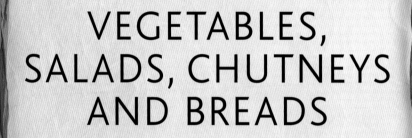

VEGETABLES, SALADS, CHUTNEYS AND BREADS

CORIANDER (CILANTRO) IS A SUPERB ADDITION
TO GUTSY VEGETABLE DISHES AND SALADS. THE
ASSERTIVE FLAVOUR OF THE LEAF ADDS SPARKLE
AND ZEST TO VEGETABLES AND THE SEED ADDS
FRAGRANCE TO PILAFFS AND FLAT BREADS.

ROASTED AUBERGINES WITH FETA AND CORIANDER

Aubergines (eggplant) take on a lovely smoky flavour when grilled on a barbecue. Choose a good quality Greek feta cheese for the best flavour.

Serves 6

3 medium aubergines (eggplant)
400g/14oz feta cheese
a small bunch of coriander (cilantro), roughly chopped
60ml/4 tbsp extra virgin olive oil
salt and ground black pepper

Prepare a barbecue. Cook the aubergines for 20 minutes, turning occasionally, until charred and soft. Remove from the barbecue and cut in half lengthways.

Carefully scoop the aubergine flesh into a bowl, reserving the skins. Mash the flesh roughly with a fork.

Crumble the feta cheese, then stir into the mashed aubergine with the chopped coriander and olive oil. Season with salt and ground black pepper to taste.

Spoon the aubergine and feta mixture back into the skins and return to the barbecue for 5 minutes to warm through. Serve immediately.

Energy 257kcal/1066kJ; Protein 12g;
Carbohydrate 4.2g, of which sugars 3.9g;
Fat 21.5g, of which saturates 10.3g;
Cholesterol 47mg; Calcium 286mg; Fibre
3.3g; Sodium 968mg.

DHAL WITH CORIANDER BAGHAAR

Boost your pulse rate with this delectable dish of red lentils with a spicy topping. This dish is also excellent made with moong dhal, a yellow split mung bean widely used in Indian cooking.

Serves 4

50 g/2 oz/¼ cup butter
2 tsp black mustard seeds
1 onion, finely chopped
2 garlic cloves, finely chopped
5 ml/1 tsp ground turmeric
5 ml/1 tsp ground cumin
2 fresh green chillies, seeded
    and finely chopped
225 g/8 oz/1 cup red lentils
300 ml/½ pint/1¼ cups canned
    coconut milk
fresh coriander (cilantro), to
    garnish

For the baghaar

50 g/1 oz/¼ cup ghee or butter
1 onion, finely chopped
2.5 ml/½ tsp garlic, chopped
2.5 ml/½ tsp ground coriander

Melt the butter in a large heavy-based pan. Add the mustard seeds. When they start to pop, add the onion and garlic and cook for 5-10 minutes until soft.

Stir in the turmeric, cumin and chillies and cook for 2 minutes. Stir in the lentils, 1 litre/1¾ pints/4 cups water and coconut milk. Bring to the boil, then cover and simmer for 40 minutes, adding water if needed. The lentils should be soft and should have absorbed most of the liquid. should have absorbed most of the liquid.

To make the baghaar, heat the ghee or butter in a frying pan and add the other ingredients. Fry gently for 1–2 minutes and pour immediately over the lentil (dhal) mixture. Garnish with coriander leaves and serve at once, with naan bread to mop up the sauce.

Energy 381kcal/1599kJ; Protein 14.9g; Carbohydrate 39.1g, of which sugars 6g; Fat 19.7g, of which saturates 10.4g; Cholesterol 27mg; Calcium 69mg; Fibre 3g; Sodium 182mg.

SPICY POTATOES WITH CORIANDER

This wonderfully spicy potato dish is popular in the Middle East. The dish can be eaten at room temperature as part of a mezze spread, or hot as an accompaniment to grilled meat and fish.

Serves 4
350g/12oz new potatoes
*60ml/4 tbsp olive oil or 30ml/
    2 tbsp ghee*
*3–4 cloves garlic, finely
    chopped*
*2 red chillies, seeded and finely
    chopped*
5–10ml/1–2 tsp cumin seeds
*sea salt and ground black
    pepper*
*bunch of fresh coriander
    (cilantro), finely chopped*
*1 lemon, cut into wedges, to
    serve*

Steam the potatoes with their skins on for about 10 minutes, until they are cooked but still firm. Drain them and refresh under cold running water. Peel off the skins and cut the potatoes into bitesize pieces.

Heat the oil or ghee in a heavy pan and cook the garlic, chillies and cumin seeds for 2–3 minutes, until they begin to colour. Add the potatoes, turning them to make sure they are coated in the oil and spices, and fry for about 5 minutes.

Season the potatoes with salt and pepper and stir in most of the coriander. (If serving the dish at room temperature, leave the potatoes to cool first.) Sprinkle the remaining coriander over the top and serve the potatoes from the pan with lemon wedges to squeeze over them.

COOK'S TIP
If the dish is to be eaten at room temperature it is preferable to cook the potatoes in olive oil, but ghee is often used instead when they are to be served piping hot.

Energy 174kcal/723kJ; Protein 2.4g; Carbohydrate 15.5g, of which sugars 1.2g; Fat 11.8g, of which saturates 1.7g; Cholesterol 0mg; Calcium 16mg; Fibre 0.9g; Sodium 12mg

PILAU RICE WITH COCONUT AND CORIANDER PESTO

A fabulous flavour triangle is created with fresh coriander (cilantro), mint leaves and green chillies in this sumptuous pilau, which can be a vegetarian meal in itself when served with a raita.

Serves 4

225g/8oz/generous 1 cup
  basmati rice
25g/1oz/⅓ cup desiccated (dry
  unsweetened shredded)
  coconut
3 garlic cloves, roughly chopped
2.5cm/1in piece of fresh root
  ginger, roughly chopped
15g/½oz coriander (cilantro)
  leaves and stalks, chopped
1–2 green chillies, chopped
50g/2oz/4 tbsp ghee or
  25g/1oz/2 tbsp unsalted
  butter and 30ml/2 tbsp
  sunflower oil or olive oil
25g/1oz raw cashew nuts
2.5cm/1in piece of cinnamon
  stick
4 cardamom pods, bruised
4 cloves
1 medium onion, finely sliced
75g/3oz/½ cup green beans,
  cut into 2.5cm/1in pieces
75g/3oz/½ cup peas, frozen
  and thawed or pre-cooked
  fresh
5 ml/1 tsp salt or to taste

Wash the rice in several changes of water until it runs clear and then leave it to soak for 20 minutes. Drain in a colander.

Soak the coconut in 150ml/5fl oz/½ cup boiling water for 10 minutes, then place in a blender with the water in which it was soaked. Add the garlic, ginger, chopped coriander and chillies, and blend until smooth. Set aside.

Melt the ghee or butter and oil in a heavy pan over a low heat. Stir-fry the cashew nuts until browned, remove and drain on absorbent paper. In the same pan, stir-fry the cinnamon, cardamom and cloves for 30 seconds. Add the onion, increase the heat to medium and fry until the onion is golden brown, stirring regularly.

Add the drained rice, cook for a minute or two and add the ground coconut mixture. Stir-fry for 2–3 minutes, then add the beans, peas and salt. Pour in 450ml/16fl oz/scant 2 cups warm water, bring it to the boil, cover the pan tightly and reduce the heat to low. Cook for 8–9 minutes without lifting the lid and then switch off the heat. Let the pan stand undisturbed for 10 minutes, fluff up the rice with a fork and serve in warmed bowls.

Energy 418kcal/1736kJ; Protein 8.2g; Carbohydrate 56g, of which sugars 5.8g; Fat 18g, of which saturates 9.4g; Cholesterol 0mg; Calcium 76mg; Fibre 3.8g; Sodium 10mg.

CHICKPEA SQUARES IN COCONUT AND CORIANDER DRESSING

This simple, delicious and highly nutritious dish comes from the mainly vegetarian state of Gujarat, in India. They make fabulous appetizers when served with chutney, for afternoon tea or party snacks.

Serves 4–6

350g/12oz/2 cups skinless split
  chickpeas (channa dhal)
45 ml/3 tbsp sunflower oil
2.5 ml/½ tsp black mustard
  seeds
2.5 ml/½ tsp asafoetida
10 ml/2 tsp ginger purée
10 ml/2 tsp garlic purée
2–4 green chillies, finely
  chopped (seeded if you like)
2.5 ml/½ tsp ground turmeric
5 ml/1 tsp salt or to taste
5 ml/1 tsp sugar
425ml/¾ pint/1¾ cups full-fat
  (whole) milk
30 ml/2 tbsp lemon juice
15 ml/1 tbsp coriander
  (cilantro) leaves, chopped
15 ml/1 tbsp desiccated (dry
  unsweetened shredded)
  coconut

Energy 357kcal/1499kJ; Protein 18.5g;
Carbohydrate 40.9g, of which sugars 5.9g;
Fat 14.5g, of which saturates 3.3g;
Cholesterol 12mg; Calcium 221mg; Fibre
7.5g; Sodium 76mg.

Wash the chickpeas and soak in cold water for 5–6 hours or overnight. Drain and process in a food processor until a fine paste is formed.

In a wok or non-stick pan, heat the oil over a medium heat. When hot, but not smoking, add the mustard seeds and reduce the heat to low.

Add the asafoetida, followed by the ginger, garlic, chillies and turmeric. Fry them gently for about a minute. Add the chickpea paste, salt and sugar, and cook, stirring, until the mixture is completely dry.

Add one-third of the milk and continue to cook, stirring, for 3–4 minutes. Repeat the process with the remaining milk.

Add the lemon juice and stir until blended. Spread the mixture on a lightly greased plate to a 30cm/12in rectangle and sprinkle over the coriander and coconut, pressing them down gently so that they stick to the chickpea mixture. Cut into squares and serve hot or cold.

BEAN SALAD WITH GARLIC AND CORIANDER

This salad is popular as a mezze dish but it is also served as an accompaniment to grilled meats. Make with fresh broad (fava) beans when in season but it is also good when prepared with frozen beans.

Serves 4–6

500g/1¼lb/3½ cups shelled broad (fava) beans
5ml/1 tsp sugar
30–45ml/2–3 tbsp olive oil
juice of ½ lemon
1–2 cloves garlic, crushed
sea salt and ground black pepper
small bunch of fresh coriander (cilantro), finely chopped

COOK'S TIP
If you prefer to serve the salad cold it can be prepared in advance. If serving warm, simply drain the beans without refreshing under cold water, toss them in the oil then add the other ingredients and serve immediately.

Energy 111kcal/464kJ; Protein 6.8g;
Carbohydrate 10.7g, of which sugars 2g;
Fat 4.8g, of which saturates 0.7g;
Cholesterol 0mg; Calcium 64mg; Fibre
5.8g; Sodium 10mg

Put the shelled beans in a pan with just enough water to cover. Stir in the sugar to preserve the colour of the beans, and bring the water to the boil. Reduce the heat and simmer, uncovered, for about 15 minutes, until the beans are cooked but remain *al dente*.

Drain the beans and refresh them under running cold water, then drain again and put them in a bowl.

Toss the beans in the oil, lemon juice and garlic. Season well with salt and pepper to taste, and stir in the coriander.

CORIANDER, COCONUT AND TAMARIND CHUTNEY

This delicious blend of coriander (cilantro), mint and coconut, with a hint of chilli, a tang of tamarind and the sweet flavour of dates, can be served with any vegetable dish or simple boiled rice.

Makes about 450g/1lb/2 cups

30ml/2 tbsp tamarind paste

30ml/2 tbsp boiling water

1 large bunch fresh coriander (cilantro), roughly chopped

1 bunch fresh mint, roughly chopped

8–10 pitted dates, roughly chopped

75g/3oz dried desiccated (dry unsweetened shredded) coconut or 50g/2oz creamed coconut, coarsely grated

2.5cm/1in piece fresh root ginger, chopped

3–5 garlic cloves, chopped

2–3 fresh chillies, chopped

juice of 2 limes or lemons

about 5ml/1 tsp sugar

salt

30–45ml/2–3 tbsp water (for a meat meal) or natural (plain) yogurt (for a dairy meal), to serve

Place the tamarind paste in a bowl and pour over the boiling water. Stir thoroughly until the paste is completely dissolved and set aside.

Place the fresh coriander, mint and pitted dates in a food processor and process briefly until finely chopped. Alternatively, chop finely by hand using a sharp knife. Place in a bowl.

Add the coconut, ginger, garlic and chillies to the chopped herbs and dates and stir in the tamarind. Season with citrus juice, sugar and salt. Spoon into sterilized jars, seal and chill.

To serve, thin the chutney with the water, if serving with a meat meal, or with yogurt for a dairy meal.

Energy 536kcal/2232kJ; Protein 10.1g; Carbohydrate 47g, of which sugars 39.5g; Fat 35.5g, of which saturates 29.8g; Cholesterol 0mg; Calcium 144mg; Fibre 6.5g; Sodium 39mg.

ORANGE AND CORIANDER BRIOCHES

The warm spicy flavour of coriander seed combines particularly well with orange. These are at their best when served warm for breakfast with plenty of hot coffee.

Makes 12

225 g/8 oz/2 cups strong white bread flour
10 ml/2 tsp easy-blend (rapid-rise) dried yeast
2.5 ml/½ tsp salt
15 ml/1 tbsp caster (superfine) sugar
10 ml/2 tsp coriander seeds, coarsely ground
grated rind (zest) of 1 orange
2 eggs, beaten
50 g/2 oz/¼ cup butter, melted
1 small egg, beaten, to glaze

Grease 12 individual brioche tins. Sift the flour into a mixing bowl and stir in the yeast, salt, sugar, ground coriander seeds and orange rind. Make a well in the centre, pour in 2 tbsp hand-hot water, the eggs and melted butter, and beat to make a soft dough. Turn the dough on to a lightly floured surface and knead for 5 minutes until smooth and elastic. Return to the clean, lightly oiled bowl, cover with clear film and leave in a warm place for 1 hour or until doubled in bulk.

Turn on to a floured surface, knead again briefly and roll into a sausage. Cut into 12 pieces. Break off a quarter of each piece and set aside. Shape the larger pieces of dough into balls and place in the prepared tins.

With a floured wooden spoon, press a hole in each dough ball. Shape each small piece of dough into a little plug and press into the holes.

Place the brioche tins on a baking sheet. Cover with lightly oiled clear film and leave in a warm place until the dough rises almost to the top of the tins. Preheat the oven to 220°C/425°F/gas 7. Brush the brioches with beaten egg and bake for 15 minutes until golden brown. Scatter over extra shreds of orange rind to decorate, if you like, and serve the brioches warm with butter.

Energy 112kcal/471kJ; Protein 2.8g; Carbohydrate 15.9g, of which sugars 1.6g; Fat 4.6g, of which saturates 2.5g; Cholesterol 41mg; Calcium 32mg; Fibre 0.6g; Sodium 119mg.

COOK'S TIP
These individual brioches look particularly attractive if they are made in special brioche tins. However, they can also be made in bun tins or muffin tins.

CORIANDER AND CHEESE YEASTED FLAT BREADS

These flat breads are salty from the halloumi cheese and are best eaten with a bowl of yogurt
sprinkled with garlic and spring onions (scallions), and cos or romaine lettuce and cucumber slices.

Makes 10

500g/1¼lb/4½ cups strong
white bread flour
2 x7g packets easy-blend
(rapid-rise) dried yeast
5ml/1 tsp sugar
1 bunch fresh chives, chopped
60–90ml/4–6 tbsp chopped
fresh coriander (cilantro)
45–75ml/3–5 tbsp dried onion
flakes
200ml/7fl oz/scant 1 cup water
60ml/4 tbsp natural (plain)
yogurt
45ml/3 tbsp olive oil
250g/9oz halloumi cheese,
finely diced

Mix the flour, yeast, sugar, chives, coriander and onion flakes in a bowl, mixer or food processor. Add the water, yogurt and oil and mix to form a dough.

Knead the dough for 5–10 minutes until smooth. Lightly oil a bowl, place the dough in it, cover with a clean dishtowel and leave to rise in a warm place for about 1 hour, or until doubled in size.

Turn the dough on to a lightly floured surface and punch down with your fists. Knead in the cheese, then knead for a further 3–4 minutes.

Preheat the oven to 220°C/425°F/Gas 7. Divide the dough into 10 pieces and shape each piece into a flat round about 1cm/½in thick. Place the dough rounds on non-stick baking sheets and leave to rise for about 10 minutes, or until doubled in size.

Bake the flat breads for about 15 minutes until they are risen and golden brown. Eat immediately.

VARIATION
For a less salty result, use finely diced Cheddar in place of the halloumi.

Energy 291kcal/1222kJ; Protein 11.8g; Carbohydrate 39.4g, of which sugars 1.3g; Fat 10.2g, of which saturates 4.6g; Cholesterol 18mg; Calcium 290mg; Fibre 1.8g; Sodium 257mg.

INDEX